THE
GREAT
ACCELERATION

A VISION OF THE ADVANCING KINGDOM IN TIMES OF GREAT SHAKING

MICHAEL FICKESS

The Great Acceleration
by Michael Fickess
Copyright © 2017
First Edition

Distributed by MorningStar Publications, Inc.,
a division of MorningStar Fellowship Church
375 Star Light Drive, Fort Mill, SC 29715
www.MorningStarMinistries.org 1-800-542-0278

International Standard Book Number—1-60708-695-6;
978-1-60708-695-6

Cover Design/Illustrations: Michael Fickess
Book Layout: Michael Fickess

Table of Contents

"The night is far spent, the day is at hand.
Therefore let us cast off the works of darkness,
and let us put on the armor of light"
(Romans 13:12 NKJV).

Introduction

The bulk of this story was given to me in a series of clear visions over the course of two weeks in August of 2016. These visions did not always come at convenient times or places. I found myself stepping into open visions during my morning commute and urgently grabbing my cell phone to make voice recordings of what I was encountering in rush hour traffic. I would be vacuuming the house and find myself in the middle of the next scene of the story, suddenly dropping the vacuum in haste and running up to the computer to scribe what I saw. In this way, the story took shape.

I also saw many portions of the book as I was writing, which made them much easier to scribe. As a night watchman on Morningstar's intercession team, I love praying and prophesying through the night. I now realize this prepared me for writing through the night. On some nights, I wrote until dawn because I could not rest until a particular chapter was written down. Next to the delight and energy that came from "watching with the Lord," sleep felt like a boring alternative. Now, I offer this book as a simple watchman's report. As you read it, I invite you to watch with me and see the same things I saw, so you may share the same sense of urgency and excitement concerning what will soon unfold.

The Scriptures must always remain our foundation for all doctrine and the first measuring rod for prophetic insight. However, the Lord gives prophetic insight to show us how to apply biblical truths to everything in our lives and the world around us, just as John explained:

"As for you, the anointing you received from him remains in you, and you do not need anyone to teach you. But as <u>his anointing teaches you about all things</u> and as that anointing is real, not counterfeit—just as it has taught you, remain in him" (I John 2:27).

In this passage, the anointing refers to the presence and guidance of the Holy Spirit each of us has received. It is no longer enough for us to activate this anointing once in a while. In order to overcome in these times and access divine guidance, we must learn to remain in the anointing continually. In context, Paul was writing to believers who faced "many antichrists" trying to lead them astray. His advice was to abide in the anointing they were given so that they could remain in the Lord. This is the same concept Jesus taught in the parable of the vine, where He proclaimed:

"I am the vine, you are the branches. He who abides in Me, and I in him, bears much fruit; for without Me you can do nothing" (John 15:5 NKJV).

The best way for us to face the future is to invest our lives in deeper intimacy with the Lord. Those who will shine brightest in the midnight hour will be those who wisely prepare for it now. If we seek His face now, we will be well prepared for anything that may unfold in the future. I hope this book will be a trumpet blast that wakes up many and stirs them to "buy oil" before the midnight hour falls (see Matthew 25:1-13).

Valuing Scripture and Prophetic Counsel

As you read this vision, you'll find it is allegorical, but this does not make it unreal. The vision reveals the spiritual realities, challenges, and promises we must consider as we approach the end of the age. If this book helps only one person prepare wisely for the decades of shaking, harvest, and rising glory soon to be revealed, then it was worth writing. Ultimately, we must "know the Scriptures and the power of God" (see Matthew 22:29) to overcome in these times. The symbols in the vision cannot be fully understood apart from their connection to Scripture.

The Bible makes it clear that we should also place a high value on prophetic revelation. Paul tells us to **"desire spiritual gifts, but especially that you may prophesy" (see I Corinthians 14:1 NKJV).** Likewise, Amos tells us that prophetic revelation is valuable because, **"the Sovereign Lord does nothing without revealing his plan to his servants the prophets" (see Amos 3:7).** The primary purpose of prophecy is to show us the Lord's plans so we can join Him in advancing the kingdom of heaven on the earth. In order to avoid error, our doctrines must be shaped and supported from our study of the Word. However, our marching orders usually come through the spirit of prophecy. The Bible tells us, **"the testimony of Jesus is the spirit of prophecy" (see Revelation 19:10).** Jesus uses the prophetic ministry to speak to His body and exert His headship over it.

Over the last few centuries, many men and women of God have prophesied about a great move of God soon to unfold. Each has contributed a unique puzzle piece—some have warned of the collapse of economic systems or turmoil in nature. Others have prophesied a great outpouring of the Holy Spirit and a massive harvest of believers around the globe. Our task is to fit these puzzle pieces together, along with the clear word of Scripture, to develop a clear and long-term plan to help us prepare. What I offer here is only one small thread, which I hope will add something to the beautiful prophetic tapestry of promises beginning to take shape for our generation.

I hope you see in the overcomers in this story those who Daniel described as "shining with the brightness of the heavens" because they are filled with wisdom and "lead many to righteousness" (see Daniel 12:3). I hope you will remember the promises of "rising glory" (see Isaiah 60:1-3) in Isaiah, even in the midst of great darkness. I hope you will contemplate the sealed ones, the redeemed multitudes, and the two witnesses of the Book of Revelation, for this story is primarily a story of the promised overcomers who will rise to meet the challenge of our times. .

Although this book primarily deals with the challenges of our times, some of the later chapters allude to the apocalyptic chapters of Revelation. I hope these sections will serve as an impetus for many to search the Scriptures and inquire of the Lord concerning what is to come. I have also created original linocut illustrations for each chapter to provide another opportunity for the reader to engage with the important prophetic messages in this book.

I am grateful to Rick Joyner for paving the way for books like this. *The Harvest* and *The Final Quest* series created new genres of Christian literature and set a high standard for other prophetic authors to follow.

Thank you for supporting Morningstar Ministries by picking up this book. Each book is the product of many staff working behind the scenes, the intercessors who lift us up daily, and the partners who give generously to support this work. If the Holy Spirit touched your life through this series or other resources we offer, we would love to hear from you.

Many Blessings,

Michael

Michael Fickess

1 | Reaching Critical Mass

The angel standing over the altar of incense wept with great heaving sobs.[1] He felt the weight of every prayer, for he was made for this task before the beginning of time. As I stood there, I too felt the heaviness. The fragrance of rich incense saturated the atmosphere and filled my nostrils. The spicy fragrance hung like a heavy cloud around the altar where it poured out in steady streams of smoke.

As I watched, I became aware of a sound emanating from the altar, like the low hum of a power generator. When I looked deeper into it, I could hear a chorus of voices ebbing and flowing like ocean waves—children's voices and grandparents' voices, teenagers, businessmen, and single moms. The sound of weeping and travail, whispering and shouting, music and liturgy, were mixed together in this heavenly place to become one sonic wave of prayer. One would expect this sound to be confusing and chaotic, but the blending of these diverse prayers produced a recognizable and steady rhythm like crashing waves.

---

[1] See Revelation 8:1-5 for the biblical basis for this chapter.

It was impossible to look upon this scene without weeping. I could feel the longing of the people for restoration, the deep desire to find the Father in the midst of great trials. I could feel the undercurrents of prayer—steady waves of love, compassion, desperation, and hope that ebbed and flowed as the prayers ascended. I began to examine some of the prayers, for each one carried a unique song and spectrum of light. Some prayers, as narrow as a strand of hair, were joined with many others to form a larger stream. Other prayers were like great pipelines that opened up wider pathways between heaven and earth.

I saw a young man's prayer offered quickly and without much thought—I wondered if it would produce any results. It formed a strand of light almost too thin to see. However, as soon as this young man's prayer was prayed, it mixed with great conduits of fire—which were the prophetic prayers of his grandmother and one of his friends. These prayers were added to his until it formed a strong and wide stream that blazed with radiant white light. It was as if their intercession completed his and was credited to his account.

In this way, there was no prayer wasted—even the sighs and groanings of the righteous were not allowed to fall to the ground.[2] I was reminded of Hannah's groaning, which allowed the Prophet Samuel to be conceived in her.[3] The slightest murmur of prayer--even the groaning for which words could not be found--were noticed by the angel over

---

[2] See Romans 8:23-27.

[3] See I Samuel 1:1-18.

the altar and joined with other prayers until they became mighty streams of light rising to the altar.

All of the prayers had this kind of synergy and beauty. Many prayers were started by one person and completed by someone else. Some prayers were begun and completed in one session, but most of them took decades—or even centuries—to complete. As I continued to look deeper into the rising prayer, I noticed the most beautiful and delicate ones. These prayers each had a unique song of restoration— songs that brought healing, hope, and comfort to other people. I knew these "most beautiful" prayers were those offered out of selfless love for others, for love is the root of restoration.

The angel did not look at me, for his eyes remained fixed on the Lord of Glory. He had stood faithfully over this altar for many generations, tending the coals of the fire, waiting. Yet throughout the centuries, the Lord's words had been resolute and firm: "Not yet…." It was clear that no one here was in a hurry, even though many of the prayers tended in the fire seemed urgent.

As the chorus of prayer continued to rise, I heard another sound, a distinct groaning that emanated from the earth itself.[4] I looked down into the depths of the earth. This groaning was marked with pain and grief, as the earth shook and heaved under the weight of wickedness. The innocent

---

4 See Romans 8:22.

blood that had seeped into the soil cried out with great longing for justice and restoration.[5]

I scanned the landscape of history and saw how the world wars and the purges of Stalin and Mao in the twentieth century caused the earth to groan with heavy travail. I looked into the slaughter of Native Americans, the cruelty of slavery, the plague of abortion, the injustice of poverty, the increase of sexual perversion, greed, and self-indulgence and saw how every historical event and social trend caused the earth to cry out all the more. I began to weep, for I could hear the earth crying out like a bound man longing to be liberated from his chains. It was a pitiful and horrifying sound. As the cries grew louder, they began to impact the creatures, soil, and water. In one especially great cry, toxic gasses were released from its fiery mantle and flocks of birds fell to the ground—this was when the soil turned to dust. For a brief time, the dust was so heavy that it blocked out the sun—this was the summer in which nothing could be grown.[6]

As I continued to watch the earth, the decades passed by like stops on a subway train. I knew we were going forward to see the prayers of the future. The prayers grew more urgent and the earth travailed all the more until we stopped in a place of pure white light.

The Lord stood in the middle of the pure white light. He turned to the steward of the altar of incense and declared

---

[5] See Genesis 4:10; Hebrews 12:24.
[6] See Joel 2:28-32.

with resolve, *"Now! Let the fire be released on the altar!"* As soon as He said this, the angel's face and body turned bright red and glowed like a hot coal.[7] He cupped his hands around the altar and breathed on it, fanning the flames. Immediately, the quality and tone of the billions of prayers rising changed. Revelation from heaven began to touch the saints in unprecedented ways. Their prayers took on the light, life, and love that flow from the face of Christ. Desperate and painful emotions were replaced with resolute faith and hope.[8]

A light began to rise, for the confession of prayer was lit up with a vision of kingdom advancement all the saints could now clearly see. Instead of the steady rhythm of ocean waves, the combined prayers now sounded like a band of trumpets and drums calling the saints to come and to prepare for war. Joy was now the primary emotion emanating from the altar—it was not mere happiness, but a deeply rejuvenating and energizing delight that flowed from an awareness of heaven's purpose. The angel smiled with deep satisfaction, for he could feel all of the excitement of the prayers he was appointed to attend.

When I looked down at the earth again, I could hear distinct voices excitedly whispering, "They're awakening! The hour of our restoration is at hand! The night is almost over!" Somehow, these voices erupted from the earth itself. For a brief time, the groaning stopped altogether, as it was overshadowed with excitement. The earth briefly forgot its

---

[7] See Psalm 104:4; Hebrews 1:7.

[8] See Romans 5:1-5; I Corinthians 13:13.

pain as this new movement of hope arose from the infusion of fire on the altar.

It was then that the Lord turned to the angel and commanded him with the same word as before: *"Now!"* From his position in the eternal realms, the angel gathered the accumulated prayers from all of human history, the great longings and desires of all the ages—the desperate cries for justice and the songs of beauteous love and restoration. As he did this, the angel burned even brighter, until he became a flame so white-hot that I could not look at him. The altar grew in size and transformed into a massive white star that burned with such heat that I had to run away from it to avoid being consumed.

I realized this great white star was a golden censer, although the gold was translucent and difficult to see from the bright radiance of the light. As the altar grew in size and took on this new shape and radiance, the angel also grew until the censer fit neatly like a baseball in his hand. Like a practiced pitcher, he cocked his arm back and launched the great censer of light to the earth. I watched it plummet to earth like a comet and braced for the impact, knowing that nothing would be as it was again.

When the censer hit the earth, it was like an atomic blast consumed the whole planet with pure white light. However, it did not hit just one time and place in history. It was so powerful that it had a "splash effect" that extended backward and forward in time. As soon as it hit, multitudes of people were impacted decades before and decades after. Forerunners and restorers of truth—even from centuries before—were raised up by this blast, even though it rose from the distant future. I could see multitudes marked in the womb and chosen for their purpose as a result of this one impact.[9] This "splash effect" backward and forward in time did not only mark the significance of what was released, but also the eternal nature of what was released.

At this point, I could no longer see the angel at the altar, for his job was done. In his place, great multitudes of angels appeared, dressed as men of war and clothed in pure white light. They descended to the earth in great companies and went throughout the earth to dress the saints in the armor and weaponry of the dawn. They held crowns and rich garments, spears and swords, scrolls of wisdom and revelation, and treasures never before seen. From this time on, the saints were equipped in a manner beyond anything seen before.

When the golden censer struck the earth, a time of great acceleration began. I became aware that this set in motion the fulfillment of Daniel chapter two:

But the rock that struck the statue became a huge mountain and filled the whole earth.

In the time of those kings, the God of heaven will set up a kingdom that will never be destroyed, nor will it be left to another people. It will crush all those kingdoms and bring them to an end, but it will itself endure forever (see Daniel 2:35, 44).

---

[9] See Psalm 139:16.

When the golden censer struck the earth, it accelerated the demise of every wicked kingdom and government on the earth.[10] The systems mankind built and placed their trust in crumbled into dust and were swept from the earth by great winds.[11] At the same time, the pace of restoration in God's people increased exponentially.[12] Next to this glorious dawn, the previous millennia seemed like little more than a dim shadow, a mere reflection of what was unfolding.

---

[10] See Revelation 11:15.

[11] See Revelation 18.

[12] See Haggai 2:1-9.

The spicy fragrance hung like a heavy cloud all around the altar where it was pouring out in steady streams of smoke.

2 | The Gathering Storm of Darkness

Next, the Lord showed me a vision of a faithful intercessor named Martha.[13] It was not the first time I saw her and I remembered that the glimpses into her life always pointed to the kinds of encounters God will give to anyone who chooses to set distractions aside and sit at Christ's feet.[14]

In the vision, the sky shone with the soft blue of early morning as Martha pulled back the covers. Although she never set an alarm, she always seemed to wake up just before the full light of dawn. It was a special time for her. The atmosphere felt clear and fresh at this time of day and she relished this intimate time spent with the Father. She had fallen in love with the deep sense of peace the Lord gave her as she prayed. Sometimes, this peace was so overwhelming that she fell asleep, only to wake soon after, fully aware that her prayers had continued in her slumber. But as she stood up today, she was aware that something was different.

---

[13] Martha also appears in *Start the Countdown,* one of my earlier prophetic allegories.
[14] See Luke 10:38-42.

As soon as she climbed out of bed, the room was flooded with an electricity that stood her hair on end. She suddenly felt fully alert, her senses hyper-aware of every detail around her. Energy surged through her, and she realized she could no longer feel arthritic pain in her body. Next, she felt a sensation of ascending above the room. She passed many other rooms on her upward journey until she finally rose above a ceiling of glass. It became the floor she stood on in this heavenly dimension.

When the sensation stopped, she could still see the room, but she was much more aware of the heavenly beings around her. A young man she had known twenty-three years ago, a man who died in a tragic accident, approached her. He pointed to a window framed in gold and explained,

"From this vantage point, we can see what is coming more clearly than you can. Still, it is surprising that more people have not seen the gathering storm of darkness."

She looked out the window and saw the East Coast of the United States. A massive storm of darkness swirled out in the Atlantic large enough to touch Florida, Maine, and all the eastern seaboard simultaneously. This approaching storm was not a result of earthly weather patterns, and its target was not the coastline. This inky-black storm was a storm of spiritual darkness, and its target was the hearts and minds of people. She looked into the swirling darkness and saw that it was fueled by hatred and lawlessness. These demonic powers were the eye of the storm, with many lesser powers swirling around them.

The young man saw what she saw and explained, "This is nothing new. This storm has been brewing here for many generations and is the enemy's greatest hope for destroying this nation. It is dangerous even to look at it for very long. Those who spend too much time analyzing it end up being swept up into it, often through fear, anger, despair, and self-righteousness. Those who allow these toxic emotions into their hearts find themselves in the center of the storm before long—for these things will mature into full-blown hatred if left unchecked."

Martha's face filled with righteous indignation. "I refuse to accept this. Didn't the Lord tell Abraham He'd spare the city for ten righteous men?" (see Genesis 18:32)

The young man looked back at Martha with a twinkle in his eye. "And that is why you have been brought here. You are known in heaven as one who has the maturity to see the storm without yielding to its power. Only those with the maturity to reject the darkness can see the rising light of this time. Now, look again."

Martha's heart was much more guarded as she took a second look. She was not sure what she would see. This time, she saw what looked like small golden stars appearing along the eastern seaboard. These stars took root in the earth and grow until great flaming lampstands were raised up all along the East Coast. She was satisfied with this remedy, for her life was dedicated to "raising up a standard" of intercessory prayer whenever the enemy "came in like a flood" (see Isaiah 59:19). She turned back to the young man.

The young man, now smiling, spoke with excitement, "Keep watching, and you'll see what you do not yet know."

As Martha turned back to the gold-framed window, she saw a great blast of pure white light. She knew it was something weighty to be released from heaven in the decades to come. Shortly thereafter, she saw the people from the region of the lampstand rising to meet in the air. They were clothed in pure white linen, as white as lightning, and they shone with the radiance of the dawn. They traveled together on clouds—some in small groups and some in great companies. The clouds would move to a particular state, region, or geographic feature and rain down lightning on the places where the enemy had taken dominion. Wherever the clouds were stationed, no power of darkness could remain or take root. No power of darkness could reach the clouds either, for the holy people were impervious to the influence of darkness from this higher position. They simply reigned over whatever region the Spirit moved them to.

The young man gave a clear interpretation. "These are the holy ones who will meet the Lord in the air. However, they will learn to live as holy ones long before He returns to join them. They will be living lightning, hearing and transmitting the voice of the Holy One. In fact, He will not return until they fully become the bride He dreams about. He will not return until a holy people learns to abide in Him all the time so that He can abide in them all the time, for only then can there be much fruit in the earth. Great wisdom and revelation will be released at this time, spiritual weaponry that can utterly defeat the powers of darkness will be freely given—but holy consecration will always be revealed first. This is why Joshua was told, **'Consecrate yourselves, for tomorrow the Lord will do amazing things among you' (Joshua 3:5).** Only those whose hearts are fully committed to the Lord can be trusted with what is about to be released."

As soon as the young man said, "about to be released," Martha saw the angels of the Lord working in the Father's armory, fashioning great lightning swords and fiery bows, preparing armor made of pure eternal light and glory with which to clothe the saints.

"Nothing will be impossible for this generation once they have been clothed in the armor of light."

The young man walked out of the room. The vision vanished as quickly as it had come. Martha scribed out the experience in her journal, using simple shorthand notes and bullet points. The last words she wrote were, "the great acceleration is coming…must add more fire on the altar… must dedicate myself to praying this through…a future generation depends on it…."

As Martha turned back to the gold-framed window, she saw a
great blast of pure white light. She knew it was something
weighty to be released from heaven in the decades to come.

24

3 | The Mountains of Darkness

The storm of darkness came as a cloud of toxic black smoke, making it difficult to breathe or see clearly. People began to collapse to the ground, their thoughts and feelings gripped by panic. As the inky darkness spread through the land, it had a sick intelligence of its own. Its putrid odor seeped into any heart or home where the doors were left open. Even those who had easily resisted dark thoughts and feelings in the past now had the sense they were wading through heavy flowing waters. It became more and more difficult to resist the steady undertow of hatred in the flow of the dark atmosphere.

Those who allowed fear and anxiety to remain in their hearts about small matters in the past now became complete captives of its power. Fear crippled them to the extent they could not think rationally or take obvious precautions. Those who harbored any racism in the past now found themselves flooded with a level of hatred that filled their hearts with murder. Families, churches, and neighborhoods that did not cultivate love and commitment were quickly fractured. This was one of the darkest strategies because it allowed the enemy to target them in isolation until each was bound with dark chains of unforgiveness, resentment, and hatred.

As the darkness settled in, fallen angels began walking among the prisoners of darkness, taking any who belonged to them. Those bound with fear and anxiety were taken to a valley of darkness marked "fear." Those who harbored any form of hatred were taken to a valley labeled "hatred." These valleys became so piled with chained bodies that they soon became mountains of darkness towering high above the landscape. The darkness now swirled overhead and the land fell under a weighty shadow, as black as night. There were now thousands of these mountains of darkness being raised up, each marked with the primary spirit that imprisoned the people at its base. The fallen angels would sit at the top of each mountain of chained prisoners, competing to see who could hold dominion over the most souls. They were drinking, laughing, and gloating from the souls they held captive.

As I began to look around, I also noticed mountains where the prisoners thought they were having a good time. The prisoners in the mountain of sexual defilement would see their painful chains only briefly, and then do unmentionable things to forget their pain. As a result, they would feel more pain, which caused them to accelerate their sins to even greater depravity. The same was true with the mountain of alcohol and the mountain of drugs. The weighty darkness drew many more to these mountains as they sought to escape the chains of fear and despair.

From time to time, a fallen angel marked "false Christ" would walk among the mountains promising liberty from fear, hatred, and addiction. They each carried ropes that shone with a sickly green light. They would offer a "lifeline" to the prisoners in one of the mountains, which would allow them to pull them out from the mountain they were in. I was surprised that many of them were released from their chains until I noticed that the people were now bound to the "lifeline." The false Christs kept walking until they had many people connected to their line, leading them among the dark mountains like chain gangs. The people who followed the false Christs suffered continually from pangs of hunger and thirst. Some walked doubled-over and were forced to continue their march despite their weariness. Instead of comparing the size of their mountains like the other fallen angels, they counted the number of prisoners bound to their "lifeline." The rope bound the prisoners to the fallen angel so that when he was thrown into hell in the end, and they would accompany him.

"They're almost ripe." I turned to see a Christian leader who had recently gone to be with the Lord. He wore a train master's vest and his beard was trimmed and pure white. In his right hand, he was holding a golden pocket watch on a golden chain.

"This is horrifying to watch, and yet you sound excited. What is it I'm not seeing?"

When he smiled in response, I felt the warmth and love of the Father. He tapped on his golden pocket watch and said, "The glory train has been coming a long time. When it arrives here, a great acceleration will take place such as the world has never seen!"

He surveyed the desperate scene again and again looked at the pocket watch. I pointed to his watch and said, "I see you have a watch there. Can you tell me when it is coming?"

He eyed me for a moment and then motioned to me. "Come closer and I'll show you."

He held out the watch for me to examine, and I realized that it was not a watch but a pressure gauge. The pressure gauge had even increments to measure rising pressure and then about a centimeter-wide section that was bright red.

He explained, "This train will not arrive until we enter the red zone, because only then will the harvest be fully ripe. I am allowed to watch its approach because I was one of the laborers who helped to reveal the track for it through prophetic and teaching gifts. Many other laborers are allowed to watch its approach because they established stations, rest areas, and connections along the way."

As he spoke, the needle on the pressure gauge vibrated just a hair short of the red zone.

"Why can't I see it coming too?" I lamented.

"Because you're not thinking big enough." He narrowed his eyes a little, and I knew he was studying me before proceeding. "Come with me, and I will show you the tracks."

He led me to a place nearby where people were digging down in the red soil of the Carolinas. They were unearthing a massive steel wall that extended many stories into the earth.

"Here's one track they've been working on for a long time. The Father buried it in this region when the world was made. The holy people and revivalists have been working for centuries to unearth just this one section."

I was confused by what I was seeing and hearing. "But this doesn't look like a track at all—it looks more like some ancient structure I have no frame of reference for."

He repeated his gentle rebuke, "Son, you're not thinking big enough."

I slowly realized that this behemoth stories-tall structure was but a small section of the massive undergirding to support the coming move of God.

In my mind's eye, I glimpsed the hundreds of other places around the nation where centuries of kingdom work had revealed other sections of the track. For some reason, my eyes were drawn to a massive track up in Ontario, which ran through Hamilton and Toronto. I realized the glory train was going to have a regional impact nearly beyond comprehension.

"Why's the track so big? It looks more like a foundation."

"This train is unlike any glory train that has come before. It will not be a small move that comes one season and leaves the next. It will come to permanently establish the reality of spiritual Zion in cities, regions, and nations. It will release a restoration too powerful for the enemy to break again. When this glory train comes, then the kingdom of heaven will be rooted in the earth, never to be removed again—although it will be greatly tested."

I remembered the prisoners and asked, "Why is it taking so long? Aren't we losing the harvest as we speak?"

"A harvest gathered prematurely will be lost. If those who are lost in dead religion attempt to disciple the great harvest about to come in, they will make them into the same kind of 'sons of hell' they have become.[15] In this way, the harvest would be lost to compromise, false doctrine, and spiritual complacency. The new disciples would quickly fall away and go right back to one of the mountains of darkness."

He motioned to the mountains of darkness. "The Father loves them too much to allow them to be lost."

When he said this, I noticed that some of the mountains of darkness were filled entirely with believers who were saved, but living their lives in the "outer darkness." These believers were gathered into other mountains presided over by fallen angels marked "offense," "false doctrine," "unforgiveness," "complacency," and "despair." There were other mountains of deception that held believers captive, but

---

[15] See Christ's rebuke in Matthew 23.

these were the largest. The largest mountain among these was "offense."

"These mountains are also almost ripe for harvest. Believers who were not discipled to maturity will have to be led to the Lord all over again to deliver them from the darkness that has ravaged the body of Christ. Once this happens, they will become holy people and never leave His presence again."[16]

"When the Father sees these mountains of darkness, these tortured captives, He sees clusters of grapes waiting to be cut from the vine. His excitement in this hour is tangible. Even the earth is beginning to tremble in response."

As he said this, I could feel the earth trembling gently beneath my feet. It was not a violent earthquake, but a gentle rumble.

The skies turned even darker, like swirling currents of crude oil. The darkness now fell so heavily that I could no longer make out the shapes of the mountains. The fallen angels presiding over each mountain vanished into the inky blackness and the whole scene went black.

I was shown a gap of about two years between when the storm of darkness first hit and the time when the glory train described in later chapters was fully revealed. This will call for great perseverance on the part of the saints.

---

[16] See Enoch 14:23.

He tapped on his golden pocket watch and said, "The glory train has been coming a long time. When it arrives here, a great acceleration will take place such as the world has never seen!"

32

4 | The Golden Threshing Sledge

I heard the train approaching before I could see it. Its horn blasted repeatedly and I knew it was quickly drawing near. Each horn blast was the sound of a million voices crying with joy, worshipping with great affection, and releasing choruses of prophetic prayer. With each horn blast, the mountains of darkness would tremble. Even though the train had not yet come, the blasts alone had enough power and beauty to touch many of the prisoners of darkness and release them from their chains.

Every time the horn blasted, the gloating fallen angels on the mountaintops lost more of their strength. Every prisoner who heard the sound and forsook their chains stripped another layer of power and authority from the fallen angels. With each great blast, more responded to its call and stepped out from the bases of the mountains. The fallen angels shrieked in pain as power and authority was stripped from them. It was not the sound of someone losing their crown or their robe, but the sound of someone whose vital organs were being ripped from his body—this new sound threatened their very existence.

At the first blast, a middle-aged woman imprisoned in the mountain of fear began weeping with joy and shouting, "Yes, I remember now! I remember the great promises of the Father." As I looked at her, I saw her as a little girl in Sunday school, pasting cotton balls on a construction paper Lamb. Now, she walked out from the base of the mountain of darkness, bringing a half-dozen others with her.

A young man imprisoned in the mountain of sexual defilement fell in love with God at the moment he heard the first horn blast. He too wept with joy and walked out of the mountain, leaving his chains behind. From this time onward, he shone with a pure bright light of holiness because his eyes were now fixed on the beauty of the Lord, which satisfied his newly awakened spiritual hunger. This newly awakened spiritual hunger immediately outweighed all the lesser desires in his heart, crushing his carnal nature in the process.

The sound of the horn blasts was so powerful that it removed vast sections of the dark storm from the sky. New constellations of bright white stars appeared and shone radiantly with each new blast. The escaping prisoners also began to shine like bright white stars as they gathered together in the spaces between the trembling mountains of darkness.

As I was wondering what would happen next, I looked next to me to find the train master again. However, this time, his vest and his garments were fashioned of pure gold. I looked at him in surprise.

"When what I sowed into in my earthly life bears fruit in later generations, I share in the reward. I am beginning to receive the reward of all that I allowed the Father to do through me."

As he said this, a bright white light began to radiate from him, increasing in brightness with every moment we talked.

The fallen angels were now panicked with pain and fear, for their place at the mountaintops was no longer secure. They all began to look to the horizon. From their vantage point, they saw a sight so terrifying that they were compelled to flee. However, they could not escape the coming terror, for they lost all strength from the sight. The fallen angels lost their voices, their strength, their power, and all authority. They lay on the ground at the base of each mountain as dead men, powerless to rise again.

I looked to see what caused them such terror and I saw a great golden threshing sledge, as wide as a nation. Its teeth were razor sharp and it demolished any mountain in its path. Its function was like the cowcatcher on a locomotive. It was designed to clear away all obstacles in its path. However, this sledge was far more terrifying and dangerous than any cowcatcher because of its size, power, and sharpness. I immediately remembered the words of Scripture:

"Behold, I will make you into a new threshing sledge with sharp teeth; You shall thresh the mountains and beat them small, and make the hills like chaff.

"You shall winnow them, the wind shall carry them away, and the whirlwind shall scatter them; You shall

rejoice in the Lord, and glory in the Holy One of Israel" (Isaiah 41:15-16 NKJV).

I looked at the tips of the threshing sledge, which slid along the ground at lightning speed. Each "tooth" was marked with different revelations from the Spirit of Truth. The largest golden tooth was called "the Spirit of Peace." This was the vanguard of the golden threshing sledge. It was positioned at the center of the threshing sledge and helped clear the way for everything else that would follow.

The sharp teeth of the sledge were made of teachers, apostles, prophets, evangelists, and pastors who walked with God faithfully and spoke the words the Spirit gave to them all the time. These men and women of God preached and lived what the Spirit of Truth entrusted to them. As a result of their faithfulness and consecration, their whole being was charged with the electricity of Truth. They shone like holy angels. They were dressed in pure white garments, but the best thing they carried was inside. I could see flames of pure bright light burning inside of them like a roaring furnace. Their faces also burned with these white flames.

When I turned to the train master for explanation, his face also burned with a pure white flame.

"Now, the harvest is begun. It could not begin until a mature remnant of believers arose who were conformed to the image of Christ—who carried His divine nature. This is because Christ Himself will reap this harvest through them. The flame we have inside and upon our faces is nothing less than the presence of the Living Christ Himself. He is still

36

the 'Lord of the Harvest' and the great things about to unfold will all be orchestrated by His Spirit working through these holy people (see Luke 10:2)."

I turned and saw the great headlights of the train approaching, not on the ground, but in mid-air. A vast body of holy people was standing on a cloud. They were holding terrifying weapons—swords, but also bows, hammers, axes, and instruments of punishment. They were fully equipped to free the prisoners and execute decisive judgment on those who held them captive. The light they shone with was the light of the face of the Living Christ, for they were each conformed to His divine nature.

This body of holy people was unaffected by the cloud of darkness, for they were positioned higher than it could reach. They breathed the atmosphere of heaven continually. The foul poison swirling over the people's heads was positioned beneath them.

This great army separated into divisions. Little clouds went out from the big one and stationed themselves over each mountain of darkness, from which they rained down lightning to free the captives. Most of these holy people began to function as angels. They would come in swift flight, snatch one of the prisoners from the mountains, and then carry them up into the air where they could breathe again. I could not see where the people were taken once they were rescued from the storm of darkness. I turned to the train master and gave him an inquisitive look.

"Come with me," he said.

The scene rushed passed us as we traveled to the next part of the train several hundred miles south of us. It had a series of golden hoppers marked, "Salvation and Glory."

The train master explained to me, "Now, the full measure of the harvest can come in because they will be trained properly. This generation will quickly move from 'justification' to 'glorification.'[17] With the great darkness that has ravaged the earth, no one can be 'barely saved' anymore. Every disciple is now quickly taken from salvation to training that leads to glorification, so that they will shine with the knowledge of the glory of God. They will learn to walk with Him continually and live their lives from the eternal realms where they are seated with Him. This is why you could not see them returning. These are converts who will never abide in the darkness again because they are being discipled to abide in the light."[18]

At this point, I heard a sound more glorious than the train blast. It was more than the sound of saints singing and declaring heavenly realities—it was the sound of angels singing so loudly that it shook my mortal body. This sound mingled with the sound of banging hammers, saws, and clanging metal.

The train master smiled at me and said, "I haven't seen this part either. Let's go together."

---

[17] See Romans 8:28-29.
[18] See John 15:1-8; I John 1:5-9.

We traveled several more hundred miles south to find the last section of the train. It was a series of cars with great golden cranes and construction equipment. The cranes worked with lightning speed, leveling ground, laying foundations, and raising up walls and towers. The cranes were continually taking people from the golden hoppers and planting them where they belonged in the city that was rising even further in the distance.

Behind the train, there was a vast and golden landscape. It sparkled with every color of light, and music erupted from it like rippling water.

One angel who was singing noticed our approach and spoke into our thoughts with great joy, "Welcome to spiritual Zion! Here, there is no more death, mourning, crying, or pain! Here, the old order of things has passed away. Here, God dwells with men continually and they have become His people."[19]

A great valley of restoration now stood before us and we found ourselves standing on its translucent golden streets. The train master left me to go his way and I began walking down into the valley towards the sparkling city. I wondered why the holy city appeared to be a valley. Then I realized it was because the mountain of the Lord had not yet been fully established in the earth.

---

[19] See Revelation 21-22.

The sound of the horn blasts was so powerful that it removed vast sections of the dark storm from the sky. New constellations of bright white stars began to appear and shine radiantly with each new blast.

I looked to see what caused them such terror and I saw a great golden threshing sledge, as wide as a nation. Its teeth were razor sharp and it completely demolished any mountain in its path.

5 | Into Spiritual Zion

Everyone in the city shone with a radiant light. Some shone with the pure white fire I saw on the vanguard of the golden threshing sledge—these were those that were completely conformed to Christ's divine nature. Others shone with a soft glow in different colors, like pure jewels. As I walked down the city street, I became aware that everyone knew my thoughts—and I could see theirs as well. It was only necessary to use words when something was particularly important to communicate. In fact, words were carefully guarded because they had so much power in this place.

A cobbler worked in front of his shop, tanning leather and forming it into shoes for the people. I wondered why anyone here would need new shoes, since it seemed like we were in heaven.

Hearing my thoughts, the cobbler stopped working and looked up at me. "Son, these shoes aren't for here. These shoes are for the ones going back out."

He set his tools down and led me inside the shop. There was a portal there, through which I could see the mountains of darkness as they continued to crumble. I remembered the people who were being rescued.

The cobbler continued, "This isn't the heaven of the future. This is the spiritual Zion being established now. You can live from this reality every day.[20] The truth is, angels already surround you all the time. You already have access to the throne room. Those who draw near to the Lord will have great peace no matter what unfolds because they will live in the light of His face all the time."

I looked around the shop at the racks of new shoes and took in the fragrance of freshly tanned leather.

The cobbler continued, "I've been through a lot in these times. Some of my loved ones have been martyred, my home was burned down, I even lived on the streets for a time—all while other saints prospered greatly. I didn't understand it then, but I learned to walk in peace because I kept my heart and mind fixed on the Lord all the time. Now, I've found the value of my trials, for I have a weight of peace that no storm of darkness can conquer. My job now is to teach every one the Lord sends me to walk in peace and confidence in God, no matter what unfolds in the world around them."

As he spoke, I realized that spiritual Zion was filled with many survivors like him who had grown through great trials so that their gifts would be refined at the hour they are most needed.

---

[20] See Hebrews 12:18-24.

I looked down at his shoes, which were blue suede wing tips. He began to sing the words of the classic song and tap his feet:

But you can knock me down,
step in my face,
slander my name all over the place,
and do anything that you want to do
But, honey, lay off my blue suede shoes
You can do anything but
lay off my blue suede shoes[21]

As he sung and moved around the room, his joy was infectious and I chuckled at his antics. He stopped dancing and gave me a serious look, gesturing to the portal that led back to the crumbling mountains of darkness.

"Make no mistake. If we learn to walk in the peace of God, we will have authority over all of this—and even have fun along the way. But those who allow their peace to be 'stepped on' by circumstances will be quickly drawn back into the kingdom of darkness."

He handed me a pair of slippers, like the fuzzy ones my grandmother used to wear around the house before bed.

"These are for you." I was disappointed, hoping to receive something tough like army boots or hiking shoes or something stylish that others could see.

---

[21] The lyrics from *Blue Suede Shoes* were originally written by Carl Perkins in 1955 and later popularized through Elvis Presley.

He answered my thoughts, "I give people what they need —which is always better than what they want. You need to learn to rest in the Father all the time and abide in His house, because that's what you're called to. Trust me, nothing else here would fit you right now. I found peace by praising through my trials, even when the world stepped on me. You will find peace by resting in the Father and letting Him rest in you. From this position, I don't know if you'll even notice the trials around you. Your eyes will be fixed on building a place where He can dwell in His people all the time."

As he talked, a bewildered young girl walked through the door of the shop. The cobbler quickly ended our discussion with a benediction from Scripture: "May your feet always be fitted with the readiness that comes from the gospel of peace" (see Ephesians 6:15) and sent me on my way with a gesture. I realized he must have served a lot of people in this way.

As he greeted the young girl, I put on the slippers and found my way to the door. I looked back to see him giving the young girl a pair of ruby-red slippers so she could learn to see heaven in the midst of the turmoil in the world. When she learned to abide in the living color of heaven, the "wicked witch" of Jezebel would no longer intimidate her as she had in the past.

Each shop featured a sign on the front without words. The cobbler's shop was marked with a shoe and the next shop was marked with an anvil. As I approached, a young African-American man walked out shining like the dawn.

He carried a great and terrible sword made of lightning. As I drew nearer, he vanished in a flash of bright white light.

Before I could approach the door of the shop, two angels wearing leather blacksmith aprons appeared and grabbed my shoulders. They had stern red faces. In a flash of light, they transported me to the armory of heaven, which was far away from the rest of the city. Swirling orange nebulae surrounded the armory, and I knew we were in some place on the outer reaches of the universe. A great anvil glowed like a burning ember, and they each held a great hammer, which shone with the same orange fire. I was afraid to speak to them because of their serious look, so I simply held out my hands to receive my new armor and weapons.

To my surprise, they placed me on the anvil. They began to bring the full weight of their hammers on my back, crushing me between the iron, pulverizing me with the blazing fire that erupted with every swing. They showed no mercy, but strangely I felt more delight than pain. Each time the hammer fell, I became aware of a dark thought or feeling leaving me to be replaced by one of God's thoughts. Each time I felt the blazing fire, I was given a clear image of a prophetic promise I was meant to receive, internalize, and carry for the rest of my life. The beating continued until I could feel no more shadow of darkness in my soul, until my whole being was captivated by the Father's precious promises that now burned like fire in my bones.

When I stood up again, they were smiling. They reached out to shake my hand as if I had just graduated and received my diploma. I looked down to find myself clothed in the armor of light, with full plates on every part of me. A lightning sword was sheathed at my side, and I could feel pulses of electricity coming from it as it waited to fulfill its purpose. I reached down and grabbed the handle. As soon as I touched it, I was flooded with the desire of the Father to touch His children and deliver them from the darkness. I felt His courage and resolve, for this sword of prophetic promises was a channel to the desires of the Father. It gave me access to what He was thinking and feeling so that I could declare His Word accurately and with the right motives. I also knew that it would tell me where to go next. Although there were many more shops to explore in Zion—I was already changed by the desires of the Father that flowed through the sword. I desperately wanted to go back to the thick of the battle after only one touch of the sword.

I boldly unsheathed the sword of the Father's desire, gripping it firmly in my hand. I felt the desire and love of the Father for the people—it washed over me like waves of electricity. I realized that the secret to allowing the Spirit to move me from one place to another was to allow His desires to completely overshadow my own desires. As I committed myself to yield fully to this flow of the Father's desires in all of my being, I vanished in a flash of light.

*In a flash of light, they transported me to the armory of heaven,
which was far way from the rest of the city. Swirling orange
nebulae surrounded the armory and I knew we were in some place
on the outer reaches of the universe.*

6 | The Mountain of Lawlessness

When I unsheathed the sword, I found myself standing in front of the Mountain of Lawlessness. However, the swirling darkness was terrified of me. I was now completely connected to the holiness of the Father—I was connected to His desire and this made me untouchable. I wept as His perfect beauty and affirming love swept over me in waves, pulsing from the sword in my hand. After my own soul was satisfied again, I turned my eyes toward the people in front of me. I saw them through the Father's eyes and with His desire. Before, I had only seen them writhing in pain and torment as they were bound in chains of self-indulgence, greed, hatred, and selfishness. Now, I could see who each one of them would be in the future. I could feel the Father's great desire to liberate them from their chains and bring them into this future reality.

As I approached the mountain, the people turned towards me and began to lunge at me, looking for a place to sink their teeth, like zombies on the hunt. In the midst of great danger, I paused and closed my eyes, feeling again the weighty love of the Father for these precious ones. I knew what I must do now and tightened my grip on the sword.

I looked at the prisoner closest to me and plunged the lightning sword deep into his chest, all the way to the hilt. As I did, I knew that he could feel the great love and desire of the Father for him, for this sword carried the full weight of the Father's desires. I knew he could see the full beauty of holiness laid out before him, for I could see what he saw— the face of the Living Christ shining in radiant glory. He began to weep tears of repentance as he was drawn into the love of the Father. After the waves of love and repentance, he was shown a glimpse of who he could be. Then, one of the holy ones descended from a cloud and carried him off to one of the golden hoppers to be trained in salvation and glory, and to find his place in spiritual Zion.

I expected the people to attack me after they saw me stab the young man. However, all those who saw the young man get delivered realized the weight of what had happened. They began to line up and wait their turn, eager to join the throngs already in the golden hoppers. It was hard to imagine a harvest more ripe than this.

After seeing the great impact of this lightning sword, I began to use it with greater confidence. As I struck the hearts of one person after another, I could see the Father smiling and the angels celebrating. As I continued to work, I noticed I was far from alone. One of the clouds was positioned above the mountain, and it rained down lightning to break many of the chains before I even reached the people. Many people gave their lives to the Lord before they were even approached. They were saved in bedrooms, on street corners, and in cafes and coffee houses as the tide began to turn.

There were also many others warring on the mountain. New reinforcements arrived from Zion every moment, and they were also dressed in the armor of light. The tide was turning as the height of the mountain was lowered with the removal of each freed prisoner. The fallen angel who had taken credit for this mountain was collapsed on the ground, rendered powerless as his bounty was taken.

As I surveyed the landscape, I saw similar battles being waged along the other mountains of darkness, which now crumbled into small hills as steady streams of people were taken to salvation and glory. I knew that we must pace ourselves, for despite our progress, it would take a long time to free everyone in the mountain. Although this story was given to me as a sequence that seemed to move quickly, it was made clear to me that the rescue of the prisoners from these mountains of darkness would last for over two decades. Although I believe the Lord can move quickly, the Lord made it clear to me that His people need to plan for long-term intercession, evangelism, revival, and discipleship.

I looked back to the golden hoppers and saw they were about to overflow with new believers. I was afraid they weren't big enough, and there were some falling out the tops of the hoppers as the pace of the harvest increased. I thought about the extra work it would take to find them again and bring them back, once we had caught up with the backlog. This problem would not be fixed until the pace in which they were firmly planted in spiritual Zion exceeded the pace of the ingathering.

The dawn now rose around us, and the great golden cranes reached the region I stood in, riding on the large metal structures I had seen earlier. They were large enough to raise the kind of crystal skyscrapers that sparkled in the distance behind them. It seemed that we had won. Entire regions now shone with the light of believers properly planted in the body where they belonged.

The storm of darkness was now overcome and nowhere to be found. In its place, the fingers of the dawn painted the sky in bright pink, orange, and yellow, fading to soft pastel green and blue on the horizon. The atmosphere was now fresh and clear, like the morning after a heavy rain.

7 | A New Challenge

The believers around me began to cheer as the light of dawn shone and the golden hoppers overflowed. They shouted, "They were all wrong! All those dooms-dayers and apocalyptic soothsayers were wrong!" They began to tear eschatology books and throw them into a pile to be burned. As they did this, I reached down to feel the hilt of my sword and inquire of the Father's desire. He was greatly grieved. I saw a glimpse of many in the cloud of witnesses weeping before Him.

I quickly withdrew from the scene in sadness as more people gathered around the burning pile, each one bringing a book from teachers and prophets who had been "proven wrong" by our victory. As they continued to celebrate, one of the false Christs began to quietly rise above them. He remained unseen to those in deception, and he stepped on their heads like stair steps until he found his place at the top of a new mountain. He began to preach, explaining that Jesus no longer needed to come back, the tribulation was a farce, and the abyss was emptied and its inhabitants overcome long ago. Given the great victories the people had seen, his words felt seductively accurate. The people who sat under this false Christ lost the urgency to save the lost—for he also began to teach that everyone was already saved by default. He was greatly loved by many, but his words were pure poison. In a strange twist of irony, he was fulfilling the very books the people had burned.

The rise of this false Christ over some in the body marked a decade-long lull in the harvest. Even the faithful saints who rejected the soothing words of the false Christ began to think perhaps God's greatest work was completed. During this time, spiritual Zion still grew and spread throughout vast regions in the earth. Many multitudes were still in salvation and glory, with many more being planted where they belonged each day. However, the golden hoppers began to empty as the pace of Zion's construction in regions was now faster than the ingathering.

New mountains of darkness now grew—mountains of deception, sorcery, and witchcraft. Although they could not cross the wide walls and gates where spiritual Zion was fully established, These were movements that sought to capitalize off the many supernatural occurrences of previous decades.

Spiritual Zion became the leader of technological and scientific innovation in this time, as believers used prophetic creativity to find solutions to some of mankind's greatest problems. The false Christ twisted these innovations to explain that we were already in the new earth. During this time, secularism and humanism began to rise again, bolstered by the time of peace and prosperity that followed the great move of previous decades.

Other mountains rose now, promising to offer all the benefits of Zion without God. They used the new technologies as proof of mankind's wisdom, knowledge, and strength. They pointed to the many supernatural events of the last few decades as proof of man's intrinsic divinity.

The storm of darkness had been easy to recognize—but the storm of false light never showed up on most people's radar. These mountains of deception grew until they shone with a sickly brightness, like a compact fluorescent bulb flashing in shades of putrid grey. A white fog rose from these new mountains, which hid the fingers of dawn from the people in the mountains. However, the white fog did not have the power to block the dawn from those still abiding in spiritual Zion—the vision was too firmly planted there to depart again.

During this time, it became increasingly dangerous to try and free anyone from the new mountains. Crowds of people would come down from the new mountains to attack anyone who tried to free the prisoners. A new mountain rose called "cowards" for the believers who shrunk back in this time. As I looked at them, I knew they would have to remain there until the next wave began. I grasped my sword and felt the Father's desire. I wept for what was happening, and I fell to the ground and began to travail in prayer. As I cried out, I discerned something more than sadness on the Father's heart—I felt a rising excitement, a sense of urgency and expectancy for something new on the horizon. I stood to my feet and opened my eyes to try to see what I was missing.

"They're not ripe yet." The train master had returned to my side, unnoticed during my time of travailing prayer. I smiled, grateful for his companionship. He was dressed in a brown monk's robe that completely covered his train master uniform.

I turned to him and protested, "No…you can't mean the glory train is coming again. We already saw the great harvest, spiritual Zion is already planted in vast regions of the earth…."

I stopped talking and realized that the cloud of false light had affected my own thoughts too. I wondered what other mindsets had snuck in unchecked.

"Your sword has guarded you from the worst deceptions, but you must be mindful even of the attitudes of the heart. Your faith has grown very weak in this season."

He pointed to the region nearest us where spiritual Zion was planted. "They're not ripe yet either. The preparation for this next move must begin soon, but few anticipate it. Those who are being trained have been hidden away for their protection."

As he said, "hidden away," he pulled the corner of his robe aside to reveal a twelve stone ephod hanging over his chest, suspended by golden cords hanging from his shoulders.

He drew close and whispered to me, "A mature priesthood is rising now in the order of Melchizedek, a priesthood that will learn to rule and reign over everything. They have been given full access to heaven's storehouses and treasuries. They will restore awe and wonder of God because they are His living witnesses. They have learned to traverse space and time, they can be hidden if they want, and they move as angels between heaven and earth and to and fro throughout the earth. These ones will never die unless they choose to be martyred."

He held out a long linen strip and I knew what I must do. I wrapped it around my head snugly, making a comfortable turban that shielded my senses from the false light. As soon as I did this, I felt an invisible hand writing on my forehead. I knew intuitively that it was marking me with the words, "Holy Unto the Lord." As this happened, I felt the decisive removal of every mindset and attitude of the heart that had crept in from the false light. In its place, I felt a burning hunger to search out the depths of wisdom and understanding, of counsel and power, of the knowledge of the Lord and the fear of the Lord (see Isaiah 11:1-2). I closed my eyes, yielding to this new revelation, and felt a weighty peace I had not experienced in a long time.

When I opened my eyes, I saw priests shining like the brightness of the heavens. They were hidden everywhere. They were not just cloistered in the regions where spiritual Zion was planted, although some were teaching great mysteries there. Most were strategically planted and hidden throughout all of the new mountains. Each wore a brown robe like the train master's, with full priestly garments hidden beneath. The people burned with the pure clear light of love, but they also had the wisdom to stay hidden until the Father moved them to step out. As I looked at them, I began to share in their love. I realized I had resented the critics, the heretics—the people who had begun to persecute and slow down the last move of God. I began to see each of them in my mind's eye, forgiving them from the heart, and releasing salvation and blessing in their lives.

I looked down at my chest and realized that twelve stones were beginning to appear and grow, framed in translucent gold.

"When you learn to love as I do, then I can trust you with My power and authority." I looked up again to see Jesus standing before me, dressed in blue priestly garments, the color of a pure turquoise sky. His turban was bright white and shining like lightning.

Although I had wept in His presence and the weight of His love before, all I could feel this time was an overwhelming joy, which came from the relief of seeing Him after the last decade of increasing hardship. I looked into His eyes, which sparkled like bright blue wells in sunlight. I saw their limitless depth and found the comfort, peace, and companionship I longed for. I found words for the emotions flowing through my heart: "Lord, I want more than a fleeting moment. I don't want just another mountaintop experience. I want to walk with You all the time." It was hard to hide the desperation in my voice.

The Lord looked into me, saw my longing for Him, and said, *"That's what I want too. But to walk with Me all the time, you must be willing to go where I want to take you."*

I remembered all the times I prioritized things over Him, all the times I felt the Spirit calling me away and found something better to do. I knew better than to make excuses.

"I'm sorry. I want to be wholly Yours now—my heart, my mind, my spirit, my body. I give You all of my life again."

He took off His great turban, which was emblazoned with a crown of gold. As He did this, it flashed like lightning. He placed it on my head. My heart began to cry, "Heresy! Heresy! This cannot be, Lord," though I was too embarrassed to say the words.

The Lord looked at me sternly, knowing my thoughts before I had them. He pointed to the multitudes of priests hidden away in the mountains.

"Unless you yield to My thoughts, My will, and My desires, you have no part in Me. Unless you use My authority and power as I instructed you to do, you have no part in Me. I am not giving you honor today, but a sacred responsibility. Honor is only given to those who fulfill this responsibility." I steadied myself, remembering Paul's words: **"but we have the mind of Christ"** (see I Corinthians 2:16).

I wondered what happened to the other turban, the one the train master had given me. The Lord answered my thoughts, *"There are rising levels of consecration in this hour. It takes time, patience, and practice to learn to give all of yourself to Me continually. It is My grace that leads you gently, from one level of consecration to the next. Those who are rising now will continue to increase in holiness for all eternity, for they will see greater aspects of My divine nature with every passing day."*

As He said this, I saw an image of the moon glowing as bright as the sun and rising over a vast ocean. The ocean reflected the moon's light. As the moon rose, it shone brighter. As the moon shone brighter, the ocean began to take on the full brightness of the sun.

The Lord explained, *"The priesthood that is rising now is increasing in radiance every day. They are beginning to shine with My glory, which is the knowledge of the glory of the Father.[22] When they are fully revealed to the world, then the people will know hope that goes beyond anything seen before."*

In my mind's eye, I saw the priests busy at work in hidden places. They were writing books to restore the ones that were burned—except the books were much, much better. Instead of approaching the mountains from the outside, where the people could clearly see them approaching and attack, they worked like a hive of bees hidden on the inside. They flamed in golden radiance and began to connect to one another within the mountains, forming holy councils that flamed with the same bright white flames I had seen in the first move of God. It was then that my eyes were finally opened to what was happening— they were building Zion everywhere, even in the midst of Babylon.

---

[22] See John 17:9-26; II Corinthians 4:6.

I remembered Daniel and his friends, who remained a holy remnant when God's people were taken into captivity. I remembered the high position of authority Esther was given so she could save God's people when their very existence was threatened. I remembered Moses' long journey towards becoming the deliverer of an enslaved nation, and Joseph's long hours in the prison before he was given authority over all of Egypt. All of these things were but small shadows next to the gravity of the mighty deliverance God was about to perform through His holy people.

I realized now that the lull in the harvest, even the great deceptions that had happened in the last decade, were a great grace given to the body of Christ. This gave the mature ones in spiritual Zion the time needed to prepare for the last move, which was now at the door.

The Lord explained, "The priesthood that is rising now is increasing in radiance every day. They are beginning to shine with my glory, which is the knowledge of the glory of the Father."

8 | The Revealing

After seeing the rising priesthood, I was filled with a great measure of hope. I felt like I could breathe again. It had been a long journey and things finally looked like they were coming together for the last and final move of God. But this was exactly when they seemed to fall apart.

A great white star was cast to the earth, releasing a blast of pure white light impacting the globe simultaneously. The light revealed everything for what it was. The sickly green light and the white fog were vaporized and fell to the ground as heavy black tar. The tar began to flow towards the low spots, taking the prisoners with it. As the tar coalesced and came together, multitudes appeared to be drowning. They had no way to escape from the grip of the thick darkness that clung to them, tethering them to the ground. This represented a terrifying level of demonic possession, far beyond even that of Noah's time. The people thrashed, shrieked, convulsed, and performed horrifying sexual acts far beyond anything seen before.

Great earthquakes, volcanoes, and explosions of subterranean water and gas now erupted around the globe. Fissures opened up in the earth, which began to swallow the tar. Hell cried out, "Give me what belongs to me!" The rivers of tar flowed towards a central point, where the prisoners would soon be swallowed. From this central point, a great fire erupted and quickly traveled along the streams of tar, but the people were powerless to escape. They flailed and shrieked in pain as the unholy fire consumed them.

This is when the priests revealed themselves. Each wearing Christ's turban, they answered hell's cry of, "Give me what belongs to me!" with **"Ask of Me, and I will give You the nations for Your inheritance" (see Psalm 2:8).** In every mountain, in every house, and in every room, they now took off their cloaks of hiddenness and shone with the brightness of the sun. The great structures of refuge they had been building in secret were now revealed at the very time they were needed. It was like Joseph opening the gates to his storehouse at the very moment the famine began.

They each shone with the divine nature of Christ, for they had spent decades being conformed to His love, internalizing His Word, and abiding in His Spirit. They had learned to love in tough times so they could continue to love when the times got tougher. The drowning prisoners were filled with hope when they saw them and the structures they built. Multitudes climbed onto the glittering refuges, which were installations of Zion on earth. This move of God did not come sweeping from one region to the next like a train. It simultaneously arose in every region. Instead of tracks being laid in a few dozen cities, there were firm foundations laid everywhere. For this reason, this last and final move seemed to reach full maturity in only a few years. This does not mean that every city became a city of refuge, but that God's people were faithful enough to give every city a clear choice in the matter. It does not mean that every person chose to accept the Lord, but that every person could see the decision in the clear light of day.

Although the priests were endowed with great light, wisdom, and power, no two of them were the same. I saw a priest who had "133" inscribed on his thigh and knew he was made of thousands of people who learned to pray in unity and live with great love for each other. This priest represented the maturity of unity and brotherly love in the body of Christ at this time. Fragrant, clear anointing oil continually poured from him. When he walked, the rivers of tar would part from before him like the Red Sea parted before Moses.

A heavy cloud of glory hung around his turban. No unclean thing could touch him or draw near the heavy cloud that shone like an orb from his being. When he approached a group of prisoners stuck in a tar pit, the putrid darkness fled from him. When he drew near the people, every drop of tar was removed from them—even from the women's hair. The priest's anointing had the capacity to identify, contain, and remove the wickedness of Babylon in an instant, much like the basket described in Zechariah's vision.[23]

---

23 See Zechariah 5:5-11.

When the priest stood near the people, they were able to experience the glory he had. As a result, they longed to join him. They clung to his robes and begged him to stay. He grabbed them one by one and took them into his chest, where they became part of him, joining in the unity, love, and glory he carried. This was a much quicker move of God because every believer doing the harvesting was already mature and dressed in white. The arrival of this mature priesthood meant that when someone encountered a believer, they encountered the Living Christ and were forever changed.

These Psalm 133 priests walked throughout the earth, dispelling darkness wherever they went. They were so confident in their authority over the black tar of demonization that they walked barefoot in the midst of it. Not even a drop could come near them or touch them. They walked slowly and calmly, often smiling and stooping over to take the hands of those they were redeeming.

There were an appointed number of those who would be saved in this last move, and the priests knew what it was. They also knew that nothing else could happen until they finished their work. I looked back at the ground and realized that the level of tar was quickly rising. It was now bubbling up from the center point where it was draining before. This caused the flames of unholy fire to spread quickly and made it more difficult for the priests to minister.

I realized the tar was quickly rising to the level of the priests' heads, although it still stopped like a rippling wall where the sphere of glory protruded from each of them. I realized that the priests had the authority to purge the thick darkness from the people and from regions, at which point it would recede and go somewhere else on the earth. However, there was something else needed to fully remove it from the earth.

Some of the priests now took in the full number appointed for their region or city. When they did, they began to cover themselves again with their monk's robes, which caused them to disappear completely from sight. I knew they were returning to hidden places and secret paths of refuge prepared for them long before. I wondered if I would see them again and if the harvest was complete in those regions—if all those who were willing to be saved had already committed their lives to Christ.

"It's almost ripe." I sighed with relief, happy to have the train master returning again as my guide. However, I was confused by his words.

"What's almost ripe? The full number of the harvest has already come in for many regions. The last three decades have already brought in the countless multitudes. The body is already mature."

"When all the people are harvested, then we will harvest the earth and the powers of darkness. God's wrath is about to be fully revealed against sin, death, and hell. This final increase in thick darkness signifies that the time for this is almost here. This is the most exciting news of all human history, for when the darkness is harvested it will be removed once and for all. These priests were appointed to redeem the lost quickly, but the harvesters for this last wave are still being prepared."

As he finished speaking, he handed me a parchment scroll. When I touched it, I was immediately taken to an immense library, which appeared as an orange cloud of glowing fire. The train master came with me. Multitudes were there, reading as they walked towards a bright white light at the end of the library. As they read and walked, they each had a light radiating from them that grew brighter and brighter with each line they read.

When someone finished reading a scroll, they did not return it to the library. Instead, they ate it. As a result, its light became infused with their DNA until their bones burned with holy light. You could tell how many scrolls someone had read by how much they shined. Some of them had eaten so many books that ancient script was written all over their bodies. These were so consumed by revelation that they became the revelation.

The walls of the library grew brighter and brighter as we walked towards the bright light at the end. They brightened from orange to yellow, then to white, then they shone as white as lightning. The Lord was seated on His throne at the end of the library, for the ultimate purpose of all wisdom and revelation is to reveal Him.

As I looked around, I realized that the priests were already before the throne in urgent prayer. I knew they were still on the earth, even if hidden. They were petitioning the Lord for an answer to the rising level of darkness. I also knew that the prophets stepping into the full light of day were His decisive answer to this petition.

As we approached the Lord, He began to appear as an open book. I heard the words echo through the room,

In the beginning was the Word, and the Word was with God, and the Word was God.

He was in the beginning with God.

All things were made through Him, and without Him nothing was made that was made.

In Him was life, and the life was the light of men.

And the light shines in the darkness, and the darkness did not comprehend it (John 1:1-5 NKJV).

I realized immediately that these were words that I had read and internalized before, and that I could only hear them now because I had read them before. I looked again, and the open book again appeared as the Living Christ, who stood up, just as a great prophet approached His throne. As the prophet approached, I could feel the prophet's great love for the Lord. It was clear He had found the object of His affections this very moment. As his foot touched the first glistening stair leading up to the throne of Christ, the Lord leaped into him and he vanished in a flash of light. I touched the hilt of my sword and followed them.

In this season, immature prophets never survived. Only those who entered the full light of the Lord, meaning they allowed Him to step into them, and they were fully equipped to deal with this level of darkness. The prophet I saw the Lord step into began to preach and prophesy continually, reciting the words of all the scrolls he had read. As he spoke these holy words, his voice was the thundering voice of many waters, for it was Jesus speaking through him. The earth, the sky, and the sea obeyed whatever he said. The powers of darkness obeyed whatever he said, for they could not resist the sustaining Word of Life fully revealed in him. He went only to the priests who had not yet taken in the full number of believers appointed for them. In these places, he brought great judgment on the powers of darkness and fully removed them from the earth so the priests could finish their task.

I saw many other prophets sent throughout the earth at this time on similar tasks. Wherever they went, they carried the **"testimony of Jesus, which is the spirit of prophecy" (see Revelation 19:10).** There was no fallen angel or demon spirit that was not subject to them, no storm or virus that could not but obey. The voice from the throne spoke through them with perfect clarity, bringing the holy words that were written before the world was made to counter every power of darkness.

From this great assembly, the two greatest prophets, who were God's champions, were chosen to guard the object of God's desire—Jerusalem. I knew it was here that the next chapter of the story would begin to take place.

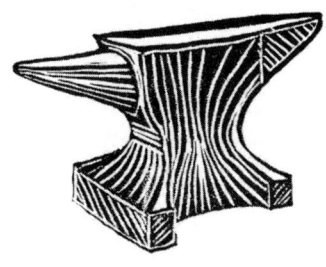

OTHER BOOKS BY MICHAEL FICKESS

DEVOTIONALS AND THEOLOGICAL WORKS

Enoch's Blessing

Paths of Ever-Increasing Glory

The Rise of His Holy Ones

The CSCL Bible Curriculum Series

PROPHETIC ALLEGORIES

Start the Countdown

The Restoration of All Things

Other titles in The Great Acceleration Trilogy

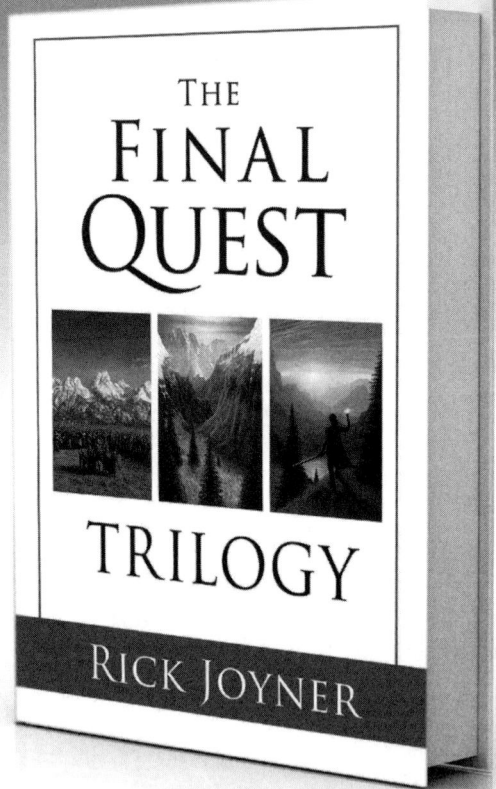

Designed to impart a balance of Word and Spirit.

WORKBOOK 1
PLANTED AND THRIVING
ON HIGH
BIBLE STUDIES
CHRIST'S WORD

MICHAEL

WORKBOOK 2
FINDING AND EXPLORING
DEEPER
BIBLE STU
RELATION:

MICHAEL

WORKBOOK 3
FINDING THE
PATH OF LIFE
BASIC TRAINING TO INTERPRET AND
USE THE SCRIPTURES FOR OURSELVES

MICHAEL FICKESS

This unique series of Bible studies is designed to help disciple students, church discipleship groups, and the multitudes of new believers who will come to the Lord as the next move of God unfolds. To learn more, download free sample lessons, or purchase, please visit:

http://mstarm.us/bible

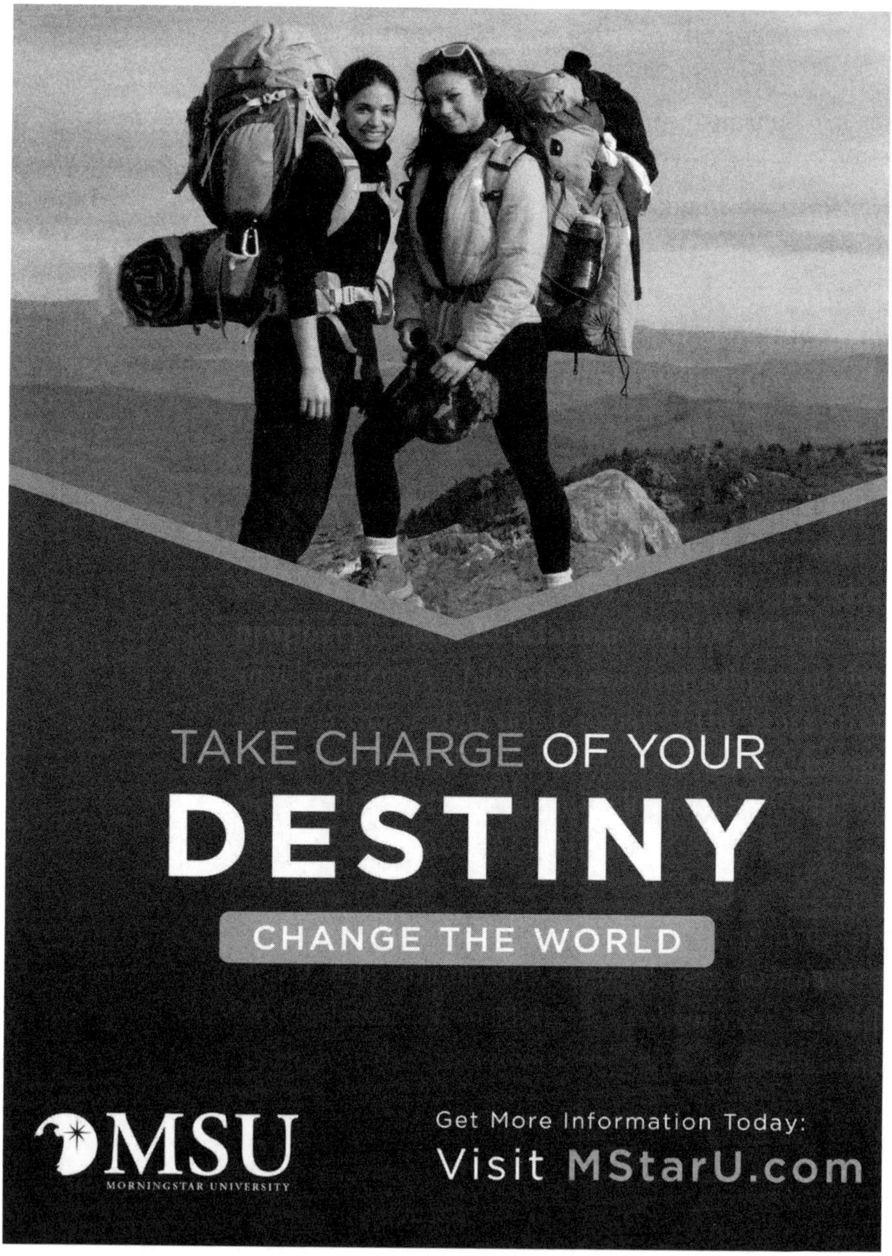

TAKE CHARGE OF YOUR
DESTINY
CHANGE THE WORLD

Get More Information Today:
Visit MStarU.com